METROPOLITAN MUSEUM OF ART.

NEW YORK

CENTENNIAL LOAN EXHIBITION

1876.

METROPOLITAN MUSEUM OF ART,

128 West 14th Street.

NATIONAL ACADEMY OF DESIGN,

Cor. 23d Street and Fourth Avenue.

(C)

CATALOGUE

OF THE

NEW YORK

CENTENNIAL LOAN EXHIBITION

OF

PAINTINGS,

Selected from the Private Art Galleries.

1876.

AT THE

METROPOLITAN MUSEUM OF ART,

128 WEST 14TH STREET.

AT THE

NATIONAL ACADEMY OF DESIGN,

COR. 23D STREET AND 4TH AVE.

Admission 25 Cents. Catalogue 25 Cents.

The present Exhibition originated in the suggestion that the City of New York ought to furnish to its centennial visitors more than its ordinary sources of entertainment. It was supposed that this object could be accomplished in no more effective way than by a loan collection of pictures. The private galleries and individual possessions of our citizens were known to be of a rare and munificient character, and it seemed probable that if these citizens could be persuaded to part with some of their treasures, for a time, a source of almost unrivalled attraction might be opened to the general public. The appeal to them was answered with the most generous responses, which enable the committee having the affair in hand to present an exhibition of art that has, they believe, never been surpassed on this continent.

The proceeds of the exhibition will enure to the benefit of the National Academy of Design and the Metropolitan Museum of Art—two of our most useful and deserving public institutions.

EXECUTIVE COMMITTEE.

John Taylor Johnston, Chairman,
Ex-Governor E. D. Morgan,
Auguste Belmont,
John H. Sherwood,
William H. Osborn,
W. Loring Andrews,
H. G. Marquand,
William E. Dodge, Jr.,
John Hoey,
J. H. Hall,
John Wolfe,
C. S. Smith,
Royal Phelps,
T. A. Havemeyer,
Lucius Tuckerman,
Charles O'Hara,
Philip Van Valkenburgh,
T. R. Butler,
Dr. F. N. Otis,
Josiah M. Fiske.
Jules Oehme,
Robert Gordon,
G. L. Burnham,
W. H. Bridgman,
William Niblo,
H. W. Robbins,
W. C. Bryant,
S. P. Avery,
William Schaus,
J. Milbank,
General J. H. Van Alen,
T. B Musgrave,
Samuel Hawk,
Benjamin H. Field,
D. H. McAlpine,
Legrand B. Cannon,
John A. Weeks,
Thatcher Adams,
Clark Bell,
Charles Butler,
W. J. Hoppin,
Theodore Roosevelt,
Daniel Huntington,
T. Addison Richards,
S. J. Guy,
J. G. Brown,
Albert Bierstadt,
F. Waller,
Thomas Hicks,
H. Peters Gray,
Eastman Johnson,
J. B. Irving,
William Page,
Samuel Colman,
W. Whittredge,
S. L. M. Barlow,
Henry N. Smith,
Bryan H. Smith,
Aaron Healy,
W. W. Kenyon,
R. M. Olyphant,
J. M. Bundy,
L. P. Morton,
George Jones,
Manton Marble,
Whitelaw Reid,
Henry G. Stebbins,
Henry E. Howland.

Parke Godwin.

Committee on Application and Selection of Pictures.

Ex-Governor E. D. MORGAN, Chairman,
JOHN TAYLOR JOHNSTON,
LUCIUS TUCKERMAN,
ROBERT HOE, JR.
WILLIAM J. HOPPIN,
PARKE GODWIN,
J. W. PINCHOT,
CLARK BELL.

Committee on Finance and Insurance.

JOHN H. SHERWOOD, Chairman,
ROBERT GORDON,
T. B. MUSGRAVE,
PHILIP VAN VALKENBURGH,
SAMUEL HAWK,
WILLIAM H. BRIDGMAN,
WILLIAM H. OSBORN.

Committee on Printing.

T. ADDISON RICHARDS, Chairman,
J. G. BROWN,
JULES OEHME.

Committee on Transportation and Hanging.

DANIEL HUNTINGTON, Chairman,
W. WHITTREDGE,
THOMAS HICKS,
S. P. AVERY,
SAMUEL COLMAN.

Committee of Management.

JOHN TAYLOR JOHNSTON,
Ex-Governor E. D. MORGAN,
WORTHINGTON WHITTREDGE,
THEODORE ROOSEVELT, JR.,
THOMAS HICKS,
J. W. PINCHOT,
PARKE GODWIN,

Treasurer.

JOHN H. SHERWOOD.

CATALOGUE.

FROM THE COLLECTION OF MR. ROBERT GORDON.

Nos. 1 to 14. (Room H.)

1 Mansfield Mountain,
S. R. Gifford, N. A., New York.

2 Winter Twilight,
G. H. Boughton, N. A., London.

3 Portrait,
Geo. A. Baker, N. A., New York.

4 Portrait,
Geo. A. Baker, N. A., New York.

5 The Chapeau,
A. Toulmouche, Paris.

6 Moorish Sentinel,
Louis C. Tiffany, New York.

7 Girl with Flowers,
W. J. Hennessy, N. A., London.

8 Artist in His Studio,
V. Chavet, Paris.

9 New Servant,
S. M. Beranger, Paris.

10 Now, I have Him,
Esbens, Paris.

11 Children at Play,

V. Mongodin.

12 Girl of Capri,

Jean L. Aubert, Paris.

13 Rustic Courtship,

W. Magrath, N. A., New York.

14 Smoking,

T. Duverger, Paris.

FROM THE COLLECTION OF MR. A. WOLFF, Jr.

Nos. 15 to 26. (Room H.)

15 Castle Knole,

Leon y Escosura, Paris.

16 Dressing for the Bull Fight,

T. Worms, Paris.

17 Rendezvous,

F. Indoni, Rome.

18 Arabs Starting on an Expedition,

Geo. Washington, Paris.

19 Soldiers throwing Dice,

A. Lesrel, Paris.

20 The Ambush,

Le Comte du Nouy, Paris.

21 The Amanuensis,

V. M. De La Fuente, Rome.

22 Mountains near Carracas,

F. G. Melbye, New York (dec'd).

23 Village Blacksmith,

Meyer Von Bremen, Berlin.

24 Sketching,
T. Worms, Paris.

25 Prisoner,
P. Jazet, Paris.

26 On Guard,
J. B. Irving, N. A., New York.

FROM THE COLLECTION OF MR. R. M. HUNT.

27 Marguerite,
W. M. Hunt, Boston, Mass

28 Boy and Butterfly,
W. M. Hunt, Boston, Mass.

FROM THE COLLECTION OF MR. B. F. CARVER.

Nos. 29 to 39. (Room H.)

29 The Wreath,
Leon y Escosura, Paris.

30 Falcons,
A. Lesrel, Paris.

31 Toilet,
A. Fabri, Rome.

32 Winter,
F. H. Kaemmerer, Paris.

33 The New Born,
C. Baugniet, Paris.

34 Landscape with Sheep,
E. Verboeckhoven, Brussels.

35 The Torn Kite,

H. Kretzschmer.

36 The Letter,

Charles Hue, Paris.

37 At the Window,

Rasinelli, Rome.

38 Torre del Schiavi,

S. R. Gifford, N. A., New York.

39 Coast View,

J. F. Kensett, N. A., New York (dec'd).

FROM THE COLLECTION OF MR. LUCIUS TUCKERMAN.

Nos. 40 to 44. (Room H.)

40 Landscape with Cattle,

Rosa Bonheur, Paris.

41 La Petite Berceuse,

H. Merle, Paris.

42 The Angel and the Child,

W. Kaulbach, Munich, (dec'd.)

43 Interior of San Marco,

David Neal, Munich.

44 Early Morning,

W. Bouguereau, Paris.

FROM THE COLLECTION OF MR. ROBERT HOE.

45 Landscape,

Alp. Wahlberg.

FROM THE COLLECTION OF MR. J. PIERPONT MORGAN.

Nos. 46 to 62. (Room H.)

46 Sale of Tickets for a Bull Fight,
L. Alvarez, Rome.

47 Love's Washerwoman,
J. L. Hamon, Paris (dec'd).

48 Marie Antoinette at Trianon,
L. Rossi, Rome.

49 Cardinal's Fete,
S. Vannutelli, Rome.

50 Pompeian Beggar,
Hector Leroux, Rome.

51 Entrance to the Tomb,
Hector Leroux, Rome.

52 The Sea,
W. P. W. Dana, N. A., New York.

53 Landscape,
A. B. Durand, N. A., New York.

54 Queen Elizabeth returning from Knighting Admiral Drake,
H. F. Schaefels.

55 High Court in Morocco,
T. Moragas.

56 A Breton Flower Girl,
G. H. Boughton, N. A., London.

57 Landscape,
J. F. Kensett, N. A., New York, (dec'd.)

58 Ostia,
W. S. Haseltine, N. A., Rome.

59 Shoe Shop,
Villegas, Rome.

60 Landscape, with Cattle,

C. Troyon, Paris (dec'd.)

61 Grand Canal,

D. Huntington, (P. N. A.), New York.

62 A Promenade in Pompeii,

F. C. Wilsch.

FROM THE COLLECTION OF MR. ROBERT L. STUART.

63 The Proposal,

E. Plassan, Paris.

64 The Foundling,

H. Salentin.

FROM THE COLLECTION OF MR. M. WARD.

65 Birds at a Trough,

F. Mery.

WATER COLORS AND DRAWINGS.

(Room F.)

FROM THE COLLECTION OF MR. J. PIERPONT MORGAN.

66 Interior of St. Marks,

Bunney.

67 Hospitale Civile,

Bunney.

FROM THE COLLECTION OF MR. ROBERT HOE, JR.

68 Baby,

Stothard, (R. A.), London (dec'd).

69 One his Eye Ne'er Rais'd,
Stothard, (R. A.), London (dec'd).

70 To Shakespeare's Ages,
Stothard, (R. A.), London (dec'd).

71 John Anderson my Joe, John,
Stothard, (R. A.), London (dec'd).

72 Interior,
Martin.

73 Mother and Child,
Unknown.

74 So the Bargain was Struck,
Stothard, (R. A.), London (dec'd)

FROM THE COLLECTION OF MR. W. L. ANDREWS.

75 Reader (pencil),
E. Meissonier, Paris.

76 Early Morning (pencil),
Eugene Klimsch, Berlin.

77 French Soldier (water color),
E. Detaille, Paris.

78 Figure (water color),
A. Boldini, Paris.

79 Napoleon at Austerlitz (water color),
E. Detaille, Paris.

80 Interior (pen and ink),
J. G. Vibert, Paris.

81 Figure (water color),
Villegas, Rome.

82 Figure (water color),

L. Leloir, Paris.

83 Fruit (pencil),

J. W. Preyer, Berlin.

84 Interior,

J. G. Vibert, Paris.

FROM THE COLLECTION OF JOHN TAYLOR JOHNSTON, Esq.

Nos. 85 to 177. (Gallery—Ground Floor.)

85 Landscape,

C. F. Daubigny, Paris.

86 A Young Roman's Bath,

G. Gleyre, Paris (dec'd).

87 In a Spanish Café,

R. Madrazo, Paris.

88 The Two Confessors,

Ed. Zamacois, Paris (dec'd).

89 Christmas in England,

G. H. Boughton, N. A., London.

90 Interior,

H. Vetter.

91 Preparing for Church,

E. Frere, Paris.

92 The Story of the Battle.

Julien Devriendt, Brussels.

93 Isabella and the pot of Basil,

Holman Hunt, London.

94 Death of Cæsar,

J. L. Gerome, Paris.

95 Spring Flowers,
J. L. Hamon, Paris (dec'd).

96 Norway Torrent,
A. Achenbach, Dusseldorf.

97 The Quarrel of the Pets,
Leon y Escosura, Paris.

98 Venus, bathing,
Paul Delaroche, Paris (dec'd).

99 Autumn Morning Landscape with Cattle,
C. Troyon, Paris (dec'd).

100 The Turkish Patrol,
A. J. Decamps, Paris.

101 Brittany Peasants at Prayer,
G. Brion, Paris.

102 Niagara,
F. E. Church, N. A., New York.

103 Scenery on the Upper Rhine,
B. C. Koek-Koek, Berlin (dec'd).

104 Temptation of St. Anthony,
L. Leloir, Paris.

105 On the way to the Bath,
W. A. Bouguereau, Paris.

106 Interior of Santa Maria,
R. Madrazo, Paris.

107 The Puzzled Musician,
Ed. Zamacois, Paris (dec'd).

108 The Connoisseurs,
V. Chavet, Paris.

109 Reading,
V. Chavet, Paris.

110 Italian Bandits surprised by Papal Troops,
Horace Vernet, Paris (dec'd.)

111 La Lecture,
F. Willems, Paris.

112 The Old Beau,
L. Knaus.

113 A Brittany Shepherdess,
J. Breton, Paris.

114 Visit to the Grandparents,
Ch. Herbsthoffer, Paris (dec'd).

115 Landscape,
Jules Dupré, Paris.

116 Improving the Eyelids,
C. Baugniet, Paris.

117 The Chase of the Butterfly,
H. Merle, Paris.

118 Prisoners from the Front,
Winslow Homer, N. A., New York.

119 The Embarkation, (French seaport at the time of Louis XIV),
E. Isabey, Paris.

120 The Letter Writer of Venice,
C. L Müller, Paris.

121 Prayer,
T. E. Duverger, Paris.

122 Industry,
Ed. Frere, Paris.

123 Watching at the Rendezvous,
T. Worms, Paris.

124 The Bookworm,
G. Brillouin, Paris.

125 Twilight in the Wilderness,
F. E. Church, N. A., New York.

126 Arabs Retreating,
A. Schreyer, Paris.

127 Settling Accounts,
J. Dyckmans.

128 Bashi Bazook,
J. L. Gerome, Paris.

129 Blowing Bubbles,
W. Bouguereau, Paris.

130 The First Cider,
T. E. Duverger, Paris.

131 Fruit,
J. W. Preyer, Berlin.

132 The new Sister,
Meyer Von Bremen, Berlin.

133 Japanese Bazaar,
E. Casters, Paris.

134 Moonlight,
L. De Winter.

135 The Slave Ship,
J. M. W. Turner, R. A., London (dec'd.)

136 Virgil and Dante crossing the Styx,
F. Delacroix, Paris.

137 Landscape, with Cattle,
E. Von Marcke, Paris.

138 The Noon-day Halt,
John Lewis Brown.

139 The Hurry for the Dress,
J. Trayer, Paris.

140 Indian Rock, Narragansett,
W. S. Haseltine, N. A., Rome.

141 The Road to the Convent,
E. Hellrath.

142 The Funeral in the Columbarium,
H. Leroux, Rome.

143 Forest of Fontainebleau,
N. Diaz, Paris.

144 Lake Lucerne,
J. W. Casilear, N. A., New York.

145 Egyptian Girl, Thebes,
C. Landelle, Paris.

146 Norwegian Lake,
H. Herzog.

147 Arrest of Franz Rakoczy, Prince of Hungary, 1701,
Julius Bęnczur.

148 Roll Call of the Last Victims of the Reign of Terror,
C. L. Müller, Paris.

149 The Cock Fight,
F. Roybet, Paris.

150 Le Massacre des Innocents,
Jean Robie, Brussels.

151 Paestum by Moonlight,
R. W. Weir, N. A., New York.

152 Herd of French Cattle,
E. Von Marcke, Paris.

153 Young Italian Mother,
Adolph Jourdan, Paris.

154 Trout Brook,
J. M. Hart, N. A., New York.

155 Trying On Borrowed Robes,
S. J. Guy, N. A., New York.

156 Tarquin and Lucretia,
W. Van Mieris.

157 Stockbridge Scenery,
A. D. Shattuck, N. A., New York.

158 The Poacher's Death,
C. Hubner, Dusseldorf.

159 Absorbed,
E. Leutze, N. A., New York (dec'd.)

160 The Crossing Sweepers,
R. M. Staigg, N. A., Boston.

161 The Chimney Corner,
Eastman Johnson, N. A., New York.

162 Railway Station, Westchester,
E. L. Henry, N. A., New York.

163 Objects of Art,
Blaise Desgoffe, Paris.

164 Greek Girl,
C. Landelle, Paris.

165 Monks at Chess,
T. Gide.

166 A Secluded Brook,
J. F. Kensett, N. A., New York, (dec'd)

167 Marine Piece,
P. J. Clays, Brussels.

168 Flemish Meadows and Cattle,
E. Verboeckhoven, Brussels.

169 Fishing Boats coming into Harbor of Brindisi,
S. R. Gifford, N. A., New York.

170 Santa Claus,
W. H. Beard, N. A., New York.

171 Winter Landscape, Holland,
A. Shelfhout, Brussels.

172 First Beach, Newport,
W. T. Richards, Philadelphia.

173 Venice at Sunset. Entrance to Grand Canal,
Felix Ziem, Paris.

174 Morning after a Fog,
William Hart, N. A., New York.

175 Wallachain Peasants Crossing a Ford,
A. Schreyer, Paris.

176 Fishing Boats at Sunset,
A. Achenbach, Dusseldorf.

177 Winter Scene in Holland,
B. C. Koek-koek, Berlin (dec'd).

178 Medea,
H. Merle, Paris.

179 Head,
Thos. Couture, Paris.

180 The Outcast,
G. H. Boughton, N. A., London.

ARTISTS REPRESENTED.

Achenbach, A., Dusseldorf.
Alvarez, L., Rome.
Aubert, Jean C., Paris.

Baker, George A., (N. A.), New York.
Bauginet, C., Paris.
Beranger, S. M., Paris.
Benczur, Julius.
Beard, W. H., (N. A.,) New York.
Bonheur, Rosa, Paris.
Bouguereau, W., Paris.
Boughton, G. H., (N. A.), London.
Boldini, A., Paris.
Brion, G., Paris.
Breton, J.
Brillouin, G., Paris.
Brown, John Lewis.
Bremen, Meyer Von., Berlin.
Bunney.

Castees, E., Paris.
Casilear, J. W., (N. A.) New York.
Chavet, V., Paris.
Church, F. E., (N. A.), New York.
Clays, P. J., Brussels.
Couture, Thos., Paris.

Dana, W. T. W. (N. A.), New York.
Daubigny, C. F., Paris.
De La Fuente, V. M., Rome.
Détaille, E., Paris.
Devriendt, Julien, Brussels.
Delaroche, Paul, Paris, (dec'd.)
Decamps, A. J., Paris,
De Winter, L.
Delacroix, Paris.
Desgoffe, Blaise, Paris.
Diaz, N., Paris.
Duverger, T., Paris.
Durand, A. B. (N. A.), New York.
Dupré, Jules, Paris.
Dyckmans, J.

Esbens, Paris.

Falria, A., Rome.
Frere, E., Paris.

Gerome, J. L., Paris.
Gide, T.
Gifford, S. R. (N. A.), New York.
Gleyre, G., Paris, (dec'd).
Guy, S. J., (N.A.,) New York.

Hamon, J. L., Paris (dec'd.)

Hart, J. M. (N. A.), New York.
Hart, William (N. A.), New York.
Haseltine, W. S., (N. A.) Rome.
Henry, E. L. (N. A.), New York.
Hellrath, E.
Hennessy, W. J. (N. A.), London.
Herbsthoffer, Ch., Paris,(dec.)
Herzog, H.
Homer, Winslow (N. A.), New York.
Hubner, C., Dusseldorf.
Hue, Charles, Paris.
Hunt, Holman, London.
Hunt, W. M., Boston, Mass.
Huntington, D., (P.N.A.) New York.

Indoni, F., Rome.
Irving, J. B., (N. A.), New York.
Isabey, E., Paris.

Jazet, P., Paris.
Jordan, Paris.
Johnson, Eastman (N. A.) New York.

Kaemmerer, F. H., Paris.
Kaulbach, W. Munich, (dec'd.)
Ketzschmer, H.
Kensett, J. F., (N. A.), New York (dec'd).
Klimsch, Eugene, Berlin.
Knaus, L., Berlin.
Koek-koek, B. C., Berlin, (dec'd).

Landelle, C., Paris.
Leon y Escosura, Paris.
Le Compte du Nouy, Paris.
Leloir, L., Paris.
Leroux, Hector, Rome.
Lesrel, A., Paris.
Leutze, E. (N. A.), New York (dec'd).

Madrazo, R., Paris.
Magrath, W. (N. A.), New York.
Martin.
Melbye, F. G., New York, (dec'd).
Merle, H., Paris.
Mery, F.
Meissonier, E., Paris.
Mongodin, V.
Moragas, T.
Müller, C. L., Paris.

Neal, David, Munich.

Plassan, E., Paris.
Preyer, Berlin.

Rasinelli, Rome.
Richards, W. T., Philadelphia.
Rossi, L., Rome.
Roybet, F.
Robie.

Salentin, H.
Schaefels, H. T.
Schreyer, A., Paris.

Shattuck, A. D. (N. A.), New York.
Shelfhout, A., Brussels.
Staigg, R. M., (N.A.), Boston.
Stothard, (R. A.), London (dec'd).

Tiffany, Louis C., New York.
Toulmouche, A., Paris.
Troyon, C., Paris, (dec'd).
Trayer, J., Paris.
Turner, J. M. W. (R. A.), London (dec'd).

Vannutelli, S., Rome.
Von Marcke, E., Paris.
Van Mieris, W.
Verboeckhoven, E., Brussels.
Vetter, H.
Vernet, Horace, Paris (dec'd).
Vibert, J. G., Paris.
Villegas, Rome.

Wahlberg, Alp.
Washington, George, Paris.
Weir, R. W. (N. A.), New York.
Wilsch, F. C.
Willems, F., Paris.
Worms, T., Paris.

Zamacois, Ed., Paris (dec'd).
Ziem, Felix, Paris.

NEW YORK
CENTENNIAL LOAN EXHIBITION.

NATIONAL ACADEMY OF DESIGN,

Cor. 23d Street & 4th Ave.

(OPEN FROM 9 A. M. TO 6½ P. M.)

The Collections at the Academy include nearly four hundred works, by the most eminent painters of Europe and America.

SELECTIONS FROM THE GALLERIES OF

EX-GOV. E. D. MORGAN,
JOHN WOLFE,
MISS CATHARINE WOLFE,
JOHN H. SHERWOOD,
CHAS. S. SMITH,
R. M. OLYPHANT,
W. L. ANDREWS,
W. E. DODGE, JR.,
THEO. A. HAVEMEYER,
MRS. C. A. LAMONT,
J. M. FISKE,
J. W. PINCHOT,
H. E. HOWLAND,
WM. H. OSBORN,
ROBERT L. STUART,
S. HAWK,
M. KNOEDLER,
EDWARD MATTHEWS,
BENJ. H. FIELD,
WHITELAW REID,
CHARLES W. GRISWOLD,
MARSHALL O. ROBERTS,
A. R. ENO,
ROBERT LENOX KENNEDY,
MRS. A. T. STEWART,
MRS. JONATHAN STURGES,
PARKE GODWIN,
GEO. A. ROBBINS,
THATCHER M. ADAMS,
PHILIP VAN VOLKENBURGH,
THOMAS B. MUSGRAVE,
H. J. FURBER,
JAS. GORDON BENNETT,
H. G. MARQUAND,
MORRIS K. JESUP,
MRS. PARAN STEVENS,
L. TURNURE,
D. H. MCALPINE,
MRS. THOS. HICKS,
W. SCHAUS,
WM. B. HART,
DAVID DUDLEY FIELD, JR.,
JOHN BIGELOW,
DR. F. N. OTIS,
ROBERT L. CUTTING,
ISRAEL CORSE,
MRS. HENRY C. POTTER,
MISS ELIZA BIERSTADT,

AND OTHERS

www.ingramcontent.com/pod-product-compliance
Lightning Source LLC
LaVergne TN
LVHW011138110826
845150LV00008B/2389

* 9 7 8 1 4 1 8 1 9 3 0 1 0 *